MASSIVE MONSTERS AND OTHER HUGE MEGASTRUCTURES

Ian Graham

QEB Publishing

Created for QED Publishing by Tall Tree Ltd
www.talltreebooks.co.uk
Editor: Rob Colson
Designers: Malcolm Parchment and Jonathan Vipond
Illustrations: Apple Illustration and Caroline Watsonw

Published in the United States by
QEB Publishing, Inc.
3 Wrigley, Suite A
Irvine, CA 92618

www.qed-publishing.co.uk

A CIP record for this book is available from the
Library of Congress.

IISBN 978 1 60992 095 1

Printed in China

Picture credits
(t=top, b=bottom, l=left, r=right, c=center, fc=front cover)
Andy Pernick 22b; **Alamy** 5b Picture Contact BV, 27 Christine Osborne Pictures; **Corbis** 4
Xinhua Press, 4b Erich Schlegel, 7 Bettmann, 9 David Gray/Reuters, 15, Charles Lenars, 16
Danny Lehman, 25 Ed Kashi, 26t Jorge Ferrari/epa, 28t Andy Clark/X00056/Reuters, 28b
Christopher Morris/VII, 31 Neil Tingle; **Getty Images** 17t William West/AFP, 29 AFP; **HKS** 6;
London 2012 18, 19; **NASA** 24; **NJR ZA** 10b; **Populous** 30; **Shutterstock** 8 Caitlin Mirra,
10t prism68, 11 oksana.perkins, 12 Dudarev Mikhail, 13 Asier Villafranca, 13c Daniel M.
Nagy, 14 Tom Cummins, 16 Gary718, 17b Chunni4691, 21 Joop Hoek, 22t Andy Z, 25
frontpage, 23 Elzbieta Sekowska, 26b Meewezen Photography; **Uploader** 23

Words in **bold** are explained in the Glossary on page 32.

Contents

Building big

People have been building massive structures for thousands of years. The biggest structures built today include dams and artificial islands. The most familiar giant structures are sports **stadiums,** which are built in cities where millions of people can see and visit them.

Holding water

Dams are barriers built across rivers and other bodies of water. When a river is blocked by a dam, the water rises behind it to form a large lake called a **reservoir.** The water pushes against the dam with a huge force, so dams have to be heavy and strong to hold back the water. A reservoir supplies fresh water to the surrounding region. Large dams also work as power stations. Water from the reservoir flows through **turbines** inside the dam. This makes the turbines spin, driving **generators** that produce **hydroelectricity.**

◀ The Cowboys Stadium, home of Dallas Cowboys football team, in Arlington, Texas, is the biggest domed stadium. It opened in 2009 and can seat 80,000 spectators.

Looking good

Fantastic new stadiums are built for major sports competitions such as the Olympic Games and soccer World Cup. Stadiums are designed by architects to be thrilling and exciting places to watch sport alongside thousands of other people. They have to look good on the outside and create a great experience for spectators inside. Even the way the sound of cheering spectators echoes around a stadium is an important part of the design.

▼ *China's Three Gorges Dam is the world's biggest hydroelectric power plant. The dam is 1.4 miles (2.3 kilometers) long and spans the Yangtze River.*

Building islands

Not all of the world's biggest man-made objects are buildings. Most of the thousands of islands dotted around the world were carved out by nature. However, a handful were built by people. Artificial islands are built to create more land for building. Homes, vacation resorts, hotels, and airports are built on artificial islands.

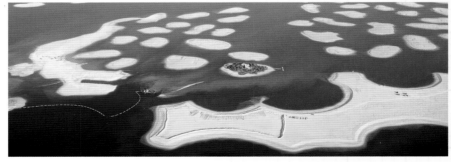

▲ *Built off the coast of Dubai, UAE, the World is a group of artificial islands that resembles a map of the world.*

Weighty designs

Massive structures weigh tens of thousands of tons. Building such big and heavy structures is difficult. The designers have to find the right places to build them, and to ensure that they will not collapse. Long before one of these structures is built, computers analyze its design, searching for weak points.

Bearing the weight

A big, heavy structure has to stand on firm ground that can bear its weight. Sometimes this presents difficulties. For example, the place chosen to build the Aztec Stadium in Mexico City was covered with volcanic rock. This rock was full of holes and criss-crossed with cracks. It was too weak to bear the 120,000-ton (109,000-tonne) stadium. About 200,000 tons (180,000 tonnes) of volcanic rock had to be removed to get down to solid **bedrock** on which to build the stadium.

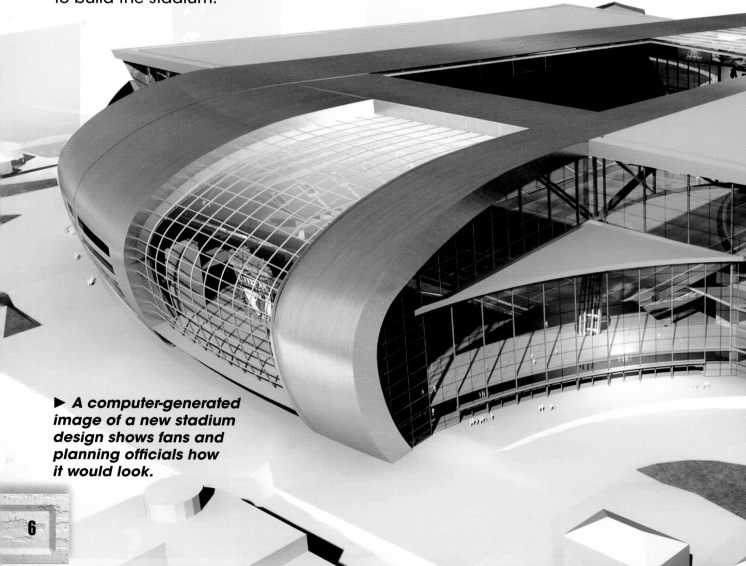

▶ *A computer-generated image of a new stadium design shows fans and planning officials how it would look.*

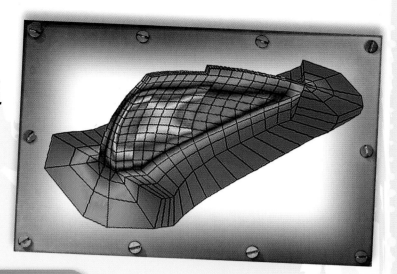

▶ *This computer model of an arch dam is color-coded to show the strength of the forces acting upon it. The red blocks show the greatest forces and any potential weak spots.*

Flooding valleys

When new dams are built to create reservoirs, the valleys that are flooded by the rising water are not always empty. The bigger the reservoir, the more likely it is that people are already living on the land that will disappear under water. More than a million people had to be moved from 1,000 towns and villages that were later submerged by the water rising behind China's Three Gorges Dam.

When the Aswan Dam was built across the Nile River in Egypt, the rising water would have submerged a pair of 3,000-year-old temples at Abu Simbel. To save the temples, they were cut up into more than 1,000 blocks and rebuilt on higher ground.

▲ *The Abu Simbel temples in Egypt were relocated when the Aswan Dam was built in the 1960s.*

MEGA FACTS

Mexico City's Aztec Stadium was built in 1966. The soccer World Cup final was held there in 1970 and 1986. Inside, there is room for 115,000 people.

Monster problems

Once a massive structure is built, it is constantly monitored and inspected to make sure there are no problems. Engineers look for cracks in large concrete structures. Cracks could mean that the ground is moving or sinking. Massive structures are so heavy that their weight can cause problems, too.

Storm shelter

When **Hurricane** Katrina hit New Orleans in August 2005, high winds peeled off the rubber outer covering of the roof of the Louisiana Superdome. However, the stadium's strong **concrete** structure held firm, and it was used to shelter more than 30,000 people whose homes had been blown or washed away by the storm.

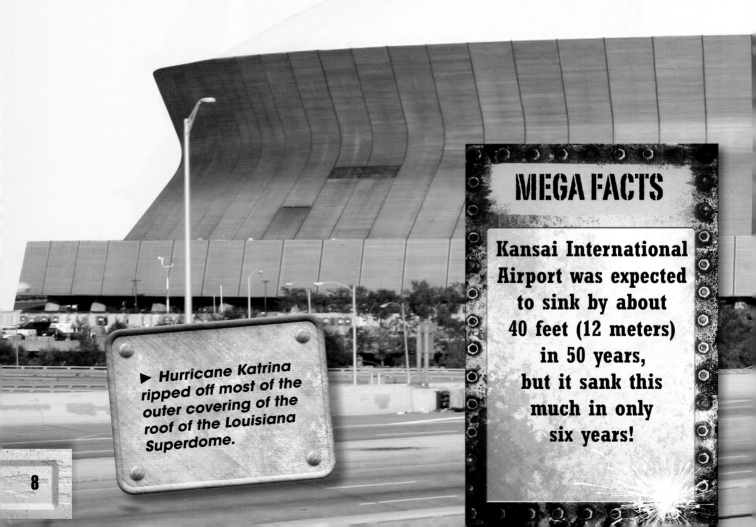

▶ Hurricane Katrina ripped off most of the outer covering of the roof of the Louisiana Superdome.

MEGA FACTS

Kansai International Airport was expected to sink by about 40 feet (12 meters) in 50 years, but it sank this much in only six years!

Causing quakes

Some structures are so heavy that they can cause **earthquakes**. Earthquakes happen because the thin crust of rock that forms the Earth's surface is cracked into pieces called plates. The plates rub against each other and get stuck. When they suddenly slip past each other, they can cause an earthquake. The weight of a dam or the reservoir behind it can set off small earthquakes called **tremors**. China's Three Gorges Dam and its reservoir have caused tremors strong enough to crack nearby roads and buildings.

▼ *Cracks have appeared in many houses near the Three Gorges Dam following earthquakes caused by the giant structure.*

Kansai Airport

Massive structures built on artificial islands face additional problems. When earth is piled up to make an artificial island, air is trapped between the particles of soil. Over time, the air is squeezed out, the particles squash closer together, and the ground sinks. Kansai Airport in Japan was built on an artificial island. The designers of its terminal building knew it might sink unevenly. They solved the problem by standing the building on 900 pillars, which can be jacked up as land sinks.

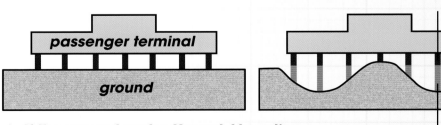

passenger terminal

ground

pillars

jack

▲ *If the ground under Kansai Airport's passenger terminal sinks unevenly, it can be jacked up until it is level again.*

▼ *Construction workers pour concrete into a reinforced structure of metal bars.*

How are they built?

Building a huge, heavy structure is a difficult task that requires careful planning. Architects work closely with the engineers and technicians who turn their design into a real building.

Getting the land ready

Once a structure has been designed, the next job is to prepare the ground. Old buildings might have to be cleared away. Loose rock that cannot be built on must be removed and the ground leveled before construction can begin.

▲ *Once the foundations of the Soccer City Stadium in Johannesburg, South Africa, were completed, its skeletonlike frame was built.*

Building strength

The Bird's Nest Stadium was designed to withstand a large earthquake.

The Bird's Nest Stadium in Beijing, China, is made of a network of steel beams. It reached its full strength only when it was complete. The stadium was supported by 78 temporary columns while it was being built. When it was completed, the columns were removed.

Building methods

How a building is constructed depends on the type of structure. A concrete dam is built by pouring concrete into a mold. Concrete is very strong in compression (when it is squeezed), but it cracks easily when it is bent or stretched. To strengthen the concrete, it is poured over steel rods called reinforcing bars, or rebars. The concrete sets hard around them. This is called **reinforced concrete**.

Foundations

Some structures are so big and heavy that their weight is enough to keep them in position. The biggest and heaviest dams work like this. But most structures have to be anchored securely to the ground so that they do not move, sag, or twist. They stand on underground pillars called **piles**. The piles provide a firm **foundation** (base) for the building.

MEGA FACTS

China's Bird's Nest Stadium was built from 7,500 steel beams. No two beams were alike. Each one was designed separately to ensure that they all fitted together.

Famous giants

The biggest structures of the Ancient World were pyramids, stadiums, tombs, and temples. The heaviest and most impressive of all was the Great Pyramid of Khufu. The Colosseum in Rome was probably the world's first great stadium, and could hold 50,000 spectators. Today, the biggest structure of all is an airport terminal.

The biggest pyramids

The Great Pyramid of Khufu was built as a tomb for the Egyptian Pharaoh Khufu around 4,500 years ago. It weighs nearly 6.6 million tons (6 million tonnes) and is the heaviest man-made structure on Earth, but it is not the biggest. The Great Pyramid of Cholula in Mexico is bigger. Today, it looks like a natural hill, but it was once a grand stone pyramid.

▲ *The Great Pyramid of Khufu (above right) is one of a trio of pyramids built at Giza, Egypt.*

▶ *The Colosseum's arena measures 250 feet (76 meters) by 144 feet (44 meters)— about two-thirds the size of a football pitch. Its wood and stone floor was covered with sand.*

The Colosseum

The Colosseum was the Roman Empire's biggest **amphitheater**, built to entertain people. The entertainment was often violent, including public executions and fights between gladiators. The Colosseum was constructed more than 1,900 years ago. It is an oval building, 617 feet (188 meters) long, 512 feet (156 meters) wide, and 159 feet (48.5 meters) high. It was built from limestone, bricks, concrete, and volcanic rock.

▶ *Terminal 3 at Dubai International Airport covers the same area as 280 football fields.*

Modern marvel

In terms of floor space, the biggest building today is Terminal 3 of the Dubai International Airport, UAE. It has 16 million square feet (1.5 million square meters) of floor space, and was built from feet concrete to fill 950 Olympic-size swimming pools. The concrete was reinforced by 500,000 tons (450,000 tonnes) of steel and a further 36,000 tons (33,000 tonnes) of steel were used to build the supporting structure.

MEGA FACTS

For 3,800 years, the Great Pyramid of Khufu, at 456 feet (139 meters) high, was the tallest building in the world. The record was taken from it in 1311 by Lincoln Cathedral, UK.

Sydney Opera House stands on a plot of land jutting out into Sydney Harbour, surrounded on three sides by water. It was designed by the Danish architect Jørn Utzon, who won a competition in the 1950s to find the best design. Utzon's winning design resembled a set of curved shells nestling inside each other.

Running late

Construction of the Opera House began in 1959, and was expected to take about four years. However, its unique shape posed a series of tricky engineering problems. It finally opened 10 years late and 14 times over budget.

▶ The Opera House appears to float on the waters of Sydney Harbour. The ground it covers is big enough to park four jumbo jets.

Sydney Opera House

year completed: 1973   length: 607 feet (185 m)

Concert halls

The Opera House is 607 feet (185 meters) long and 394 feet (120 meters) wide. It has two main auditoriums (theaters) and three smaller ones. The largest auditorium holds more than 2,650 people.

Construction

The building was constructed in three stages. Stage one involved building the foundations with a vast concrete platform on top. A total of 580 concrete piers were driven into the harbor floor. Stage two involved building the shell-like roofs. These were made from 2,194 concrete sections weighing up to 17 tons (15.5 tonnes) each. It took eight years to design and build the roofs. Stage three involved finishing the interior of the building.

▲ *The Opera House nears completion in 1971. The concrete piers that bear its weight are visible underneath it.*

MEGA FACTS

Sydney Opera House uses 20 gigawatt hours of electricity a year—as much as a town of 25,000 people.

Taking shape

Concrete was laid to make the base of the bowl and the floor of the lower **tier** of seats. More than 100 columns, each 16 feet (5 meters) high, were built to support the stadium's structure. The lower seating tier contains 25,000 seats. The upper structure contains a higher tier of 55,000 seats. A fabric curtain surrounds the stadium and provides extra protection for the spectators from the weather. Above the spectators' heads, a 92-foot-wide (28 meter) roof made of lightweight plastic fabric is held up by cables. Above the roof are 14 lighting towers.

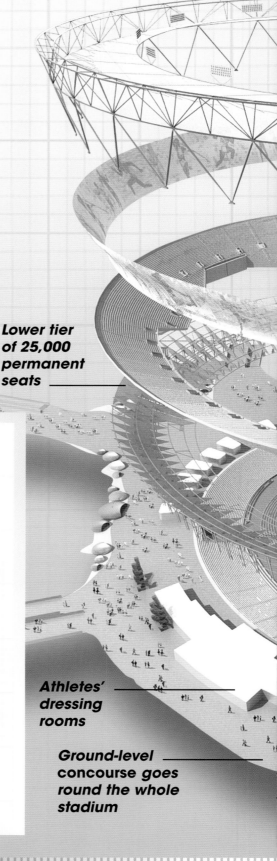

Lower tier of 25,000 permanent seats _____

Athletes' dressing rooms _____

Ground-level concourse goes round the whole stadium _____

Steel skeleton

By 2009, cranes towered over the construction site of the Olympic stadium. **Tower cranes** and mobile cranes worked together to lift the steel skeleton into position.

▲ *In November 2009, the concrete bowl that forms the base of the stadium was almost complete.*

When London was awarded the 2012 Olympic Games in 2005, a seven-year countdown began. When the clock reaches zero, in July 2012, the Games begin. By then, London's new Olympic stadium has to be designed, built, and tested. The design was unveiled in November 2007. It showed a bowl-shaped stadium partly sunk into the ground. The chosen site was an island between rivers in Stratford in northeast London.

Firm foundations

Construction of the 80,000-seat stadium began in April 2008. More than 880,000 tons (800,000 tonnes) of soil were removed from the site, and the first of 4,000 piles, each 82 feet (25 meters) deep, were sunk into the ground to form a solid foundation. The ground at one end of the stadium is higher than the other end. This slope was used in the stadium's design. Athletes' changing rooms, treatment rooms, offices, and rooms for the world's journalists and broadcasters were hidden underground at the end of the stadium where the ground is higher.

▼ *By September 2010, the basic structure of the stadium was complete. The lighting towers had been installed. Work on the field had begun.*

London's Olympic stadium

capacity: 80,000   height: 174 feet (53 m)

Sports stadiums

Sports stadiums are among the biggest and most impressive buildings constructed today. Each stadium is a one-off, specially designed for its home city. A stadium is a status symbol for the city, as well as being a functional building, where spectators can enjoy their favorite sport.

Clear view

Every spectator wants to have a clear view of every part of the playing surface or running track. Pillars would spoil their view—but without pillars, how does the roof stay up? The solution is to hold it up from above, hanging it from cables or metal struts. In most stadiums, the roof covers only the spectators, not the playing surface.

Domes

In parts of the world where storms are common, such as the southern states of the USA, stadiums may have to be completely covered during sports events to keep out extreme weather. In the 1960s and 1970s, stadiums covered with a domed roof were built. These roofs did not open at all.

▲ *The Houston Astrodome, which opened in 1965, was the world's first domed stadium.*

MEGA FACTS

The Allianz Arena (above) in Munich, Germany, is covered with plastic panels that can be lit up in different colors.

▼ *The Etihad Stadium in Melbourne, Australia, has a sliding roof. Its seating can be arranged to form a rectangle or an oval to suit different sports.*

Green grass

Most stadiums have a playing surface made of grass. The grass needs plenty of light to keep it green and healthy, but a roof cuts down the amount of light reaching the grass. Even a roof that covers only the spectators cuts down the sunlight. One answer is to make part of the roof able to move. A movable roof can cover spectators during bad weather, but between events it can be opened up to let in more light. The roof on the south side of Wembley Stadium, London, UK, slides back to let more light onto the field.

▲ *The giant arch that holds up Wembley Stadium's roof weighs 1,930 tons (1,750 tonnes)— as much as 500 fully laden trucks.*

Setting records

The roof reduces wind speeds inside the stadium. This is important, because world records in some events can be set only if the wind is below a certain speed. The designers tested models of the stadium with wind blowing from different directions to measure the wind speeds at ground level.

▲ *The stadium has been designed to hold all the track and field events in addition to the opening and closing ceremonies.*

▲ *The stadium is designed as a series of layers and rings one above the other, from the foundations up to the lighting towers.*

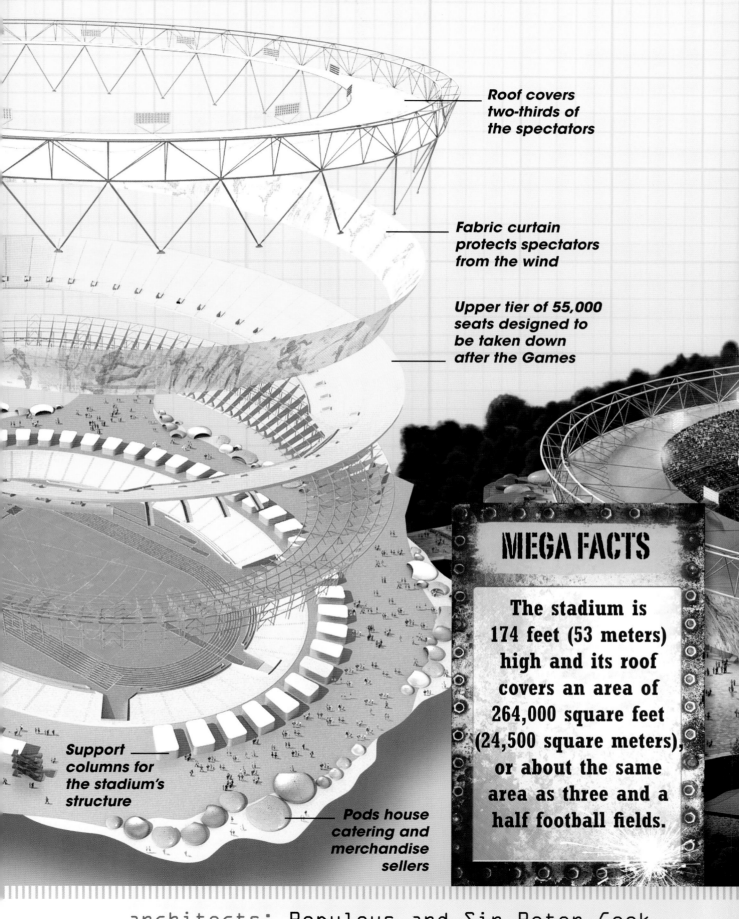

Roof covers two-thirds of the spectators

Fabric curtain protects spectators from the wind

Upper tier of 55,000 seats designed to be taken down after the Games

Support columns for the stadium's structure

Pods house catering and merchandise sellers

MEGA FACTS

The stadium is 174 feet (53 meters) high and its roof covers an area of 264,000 square feet (24,500 square meters), or about the same area as three and a half football fields.

architects: Populous and Sir Peter Cook

Dams

Dams are massive structures built across rivers and other bodies of water. There are three main types of dam: arch dams, embankment dams, and gravity dams. The choice of dam depends on the amount of water to be held back, the shape and type of the surrounding ground, and the cost of construction.

Arch dams

An arch dam is a curved wall made of reinforced concrete. It is a bit like an arched bridge lying on its side. The great weight of water pressing against the wall tries to push the ends of the wall outwards. The ends must be firmly anchored in position so that they cannot move. The ideal place for an arch dam is a narrow **canyon** with steep walls of rock on each side. An arch dam can have just one arch, or it can be built from a series of arches. The Daniel-Johnson Dam in Quebec, Canada, is an arch dam with 13 arches.

Gravity dams

A gravity dam stays in place because of its weight and shape. Gravity dams are made from concrete or stone. They can be built in the shape of arch dams and this type of dam is called an arch-gravity dam. The Hoover Dam between Arizona and Nevada is an example of an arch-gravity dam.

Embankment dams

Embankment dams rely on their weight to resist the force of water pushing against them. Embankment dams are made of **compacted** earth. To stop water seeping through, there is a layer of waterproof material on top of the dam or inside it. The waterproof material might be concrete, steel, or plastic.

▼ To produce electricity, water from the reservoir behind a dam is channeled through pipes, called penstocks, to a turbine. The force of the water spins the turbine.

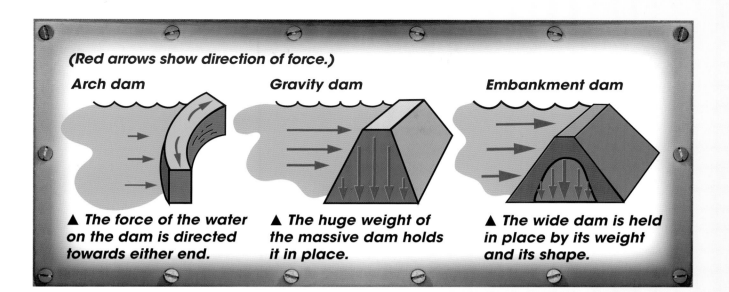

(Red arrows show direction of force.)

Arch dam

▲ The force of the water on the dam is directed towards either end.

Gravity dam

▲ The huge weight of the massive dam holds it in place.

Embankment dam

▲ The wide dam is held in place by its weight and its shape.

Afsluitdijk

One of the most ambitious dams ever built is the Afsluitdijk in the Netherlands. It is an embankment dam, and spans the mouth of the Zuiderzee, an inlet of the North Sea. The Afsluitdijk changed part of the Zuiderzee to a vast freshwater lake, called the IJsselmeer.

▲ The Afsluitdijk was built between 1927 and 1933. It is 20 miles (32 kilometers) long and 295 feet (90 meters) wide.

21

In the 1920s, the US government decided to build a dam across the Colorado River on the border of Arizona and Nevada. It was to be a massive, concrete arch-gravity dam.

Diverting the river

First, the course of the Colorado River had to be changed so that it flowed around the part of the river bed where the dam was to be built. This was done by blasting four tunnels through the walls of the Black Canyon.

The first concrete was poured in June 1933. The dam could not be made in one seamless block, because the concrete would have cracked as it set. Instead, the concrete was poured into molds that formed blocks up to 160 feet and 5 feet high. The blocks contained pipes. Chilled water was pumped through the pipes to make the concrete set more slowly and evenly to avoid cracking. Then the pipes were filled with **grout**. The vast concrete wall of the dam was finished in May 1935.

◄ *The curved wall of the Hoover Dam seen here before Lake Mead had been created. The whole dam weighs nearly 6.6 million tons (6 million tonnes).*

The Hoover Dam

length: 1,243 feet (379 m)   height: 727 feet (201 m)

Powerhouse

The last part of the dam to be built was the **powerhouse**, where electricity would be generated. The tunnels were blocked, so the Colorado River followed its natural course again. A new lake called Lake Mead filled up behind the dam. When the water was deep enough, it entered four tall intake towers and flowed through the turbines. The spinning turbines powered the electricity generators.

▲ *A row of huge turbines spin in the powerhouse.*

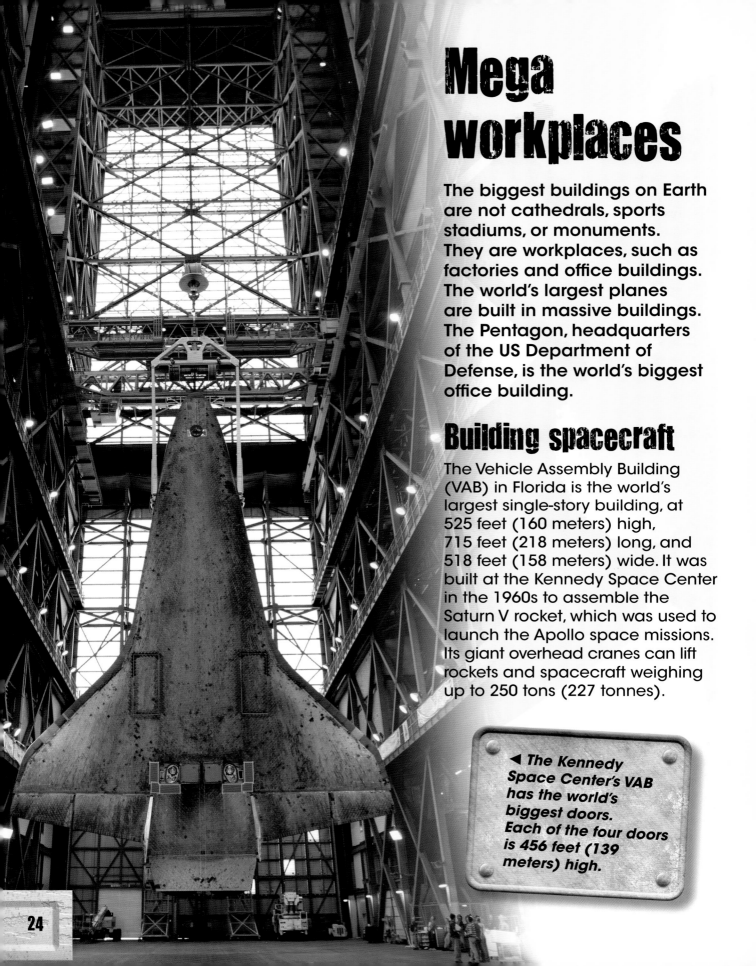

Mega workplaces

The biggest buildings on Earth are not cathedrals, sports stadiums, or monuments. They are workplaces, such as factories and office buildings. The world's largest planes are built in massive buildings. The Pentagon, headquarters of the US Department of Defense, is the world's biggest office building.

Building spacecraft

The Vehicle Assembly Building (VAB) in Florida is the world's largest single-story building, at 525 feet (160 meters) high, 715 feet (218 meters) long, and 518 feet (158 meters) wide. It was built at the Kennedy Space Center in the 1960s to assemble the Saturn V rocket, which was used to launch the Apollo space missions. Its giant overhead cranes can lift rockets and spacecraft weighing up to 250 tons (227 tonnes).

◄ *The Kennedy Space Center's VAB has the world's biggest doors. Each of the four doors is 456 feet (139 meters) high.*

Mega factory

Boeing's airliner factory in Everett, Washington State is the world's largest building by volume (the amount of space inside it). It is more than twice the size of the next biggest—the factory in France that builds the world's biggest airliner, the Airbus A380. The Everett factory covers 470 million cubic feet (13.3 million cubic meters)—the whole of Disneyland could fit inside with room to spare.

▲ *Thirty thousand people work at Boeing's Everett assembly plant, the biggest factory in the world.*

The Pentagon

The Pentagon is the world's biggest office building by floor area. It is 6.5 million square feet (604,000 square meters). About 23,000 people work in the Pentagon, which was named because of its five-sided shape. It has five floors above ground level and another two below ground. It was built during World War II (1939–45). Steel was in short supply then, so the Pentagon's concrete structure was reinforced with as little steel as possible.

▲ *Because of its shape, it takes no more than seven minutes to walk between any two offices in the Pentagon.*

MEGA FACTS

The Kennedy Space Center's Vehicle Assembly Building is designed to withstand hurricane-force winds. It stands on 4,225 steel piles.

Artificial islands

People started making artificial islands in the Stone Age, thousands of years ago. Small islands were constructed by piling up rock and earth in shallow water. Compared to the hand-built islands of past times, today's artificial islands are monsters. They are built to provide new land for homes, hotels, and airports.

▼ *The artificial Palm Islands in Dubai, UAE, are made of sand. A circular breakwater made of rock, protects them from the waves.*

Polders

The Dutch are the masters of reclaiming land from the sea and lakes. The area to be reclaimed is enclosed by building an embankment called a dyke. Then the water is pumped out to leave dry land. Land reclaimed like this is called a polder. The Dutch have created more than 3,000 polders in the past 1,000 years.

The new land created by polders is very flat. With no hills to break the wind, they are ideal for windmills.

Palm Islands

Three artificial islands have been built off the coast of Dubai. They are the Palm Jumeirah, the Palm Jebel Ali, and the Palm Deira. They are called the Palm Islands because they are shaped like palm trees.

▼ *A dredger sprays sand to create one of the artificial islands that form the World. The water depth is up to 56 feet (17 meters) and each island stands 10 feet (3 meters) above sea level.*

MEGA FACTS

The world's biggest artificial island is Flevopolder in the Netherlands. It covers an area of 375 square miles (970 square kilometers).

The World

The Palm Islands are not the only artificial islands off the Dubai coast. The World is a cluster of islands made in the shape of a map of the world. The whole "map" measures almost 4 miles (6 kilometers) by 5.6 miles (9 kilometers). Hotels and homes are being built on the islands.

Failures and accidents

The world's biggest structures are usually very safe, but occasionally things go wrong. Dams and stadiums are massive structures, but the forces of nature are strong enough to find weak points in their materials or design, sometimes with disastrous effects.

When the wind tore a hole in the roof of the BC Place Stadium in Vancouver, Canada, a worker likened the sound to "elephants running through your living room."

Buckling steel

The concrete and steel structure of a sports stadium has lighting, video screens, television cameras, loudspeakers, and all sorts of other equipment attached to it. In 1995, while the Centennial Olympic Stadium in Atlanta, Georgia, was being built, the steel beams holding up a huge tower of lights collapsed, killing a construction worker.

Flood damage

In 2009, heavy rains caused an unusually high build-up of water behind the Situ Gintung Dam in Indonesia. The dam gave way, and a wall of water rushed down the valley below. Dozens of people died in the flood.

The low-lying coastal city of New Orleans is protected from flooding by earth banks called **levees**. When Hurricane Katrina struck the city in 2005, its levees and flood walls failed in more than 50 places, letting huge amounts of water into the city. Nearly 1,500 people died.

The roof

A stadium's roof can be its weakest point. In 2009, a year after the new Sultan Mizan Zainal Abidin Stadium in Malaysia was completed, part of the roof collapsed. The sound it made was so loud that stadium workers thought a plane from a nearby airport had crashed.

▲ *The roof of the Sultan Mizan Stadium collapsed onto the spectator stand when its steel supports buckled and folded.*

▲ *After the levees broken by Hurricane Katrina had been rebuilt, water had to be pumped out of the flooded parts of New Orleans.*

Future monsters

International sports events such as the Olympic Games and the soccer World Cup are held in a different city each time. Fantastic new sports stadiums are built for each event.

The huge cost of building and operating new stadiums means that designers have to make the best use of the land. In the past, stadiums lay empty between sports events. Today's stadiums are built along with shops, offices, hotels, restaurants, and homes, so that they are busy all the time.

◄ *The new stadium for French football team Olympique Lyonnais, has been designed to have a large, glowing roof that changes color.*

Multi-purpose stadiums

Many stadiums built today are designed for one sport only—such as soccer, baseball, or athletics. Future stadiums will be able to change their playing surface more easily so that different sports can be played. The lowest layer of seats might be able to slide back to reveal a running track. A grass football field can be built in sections and these might be slid outside to reveal a hard surface for pop concerts or even motor sports.

▼ *The 40,000-seater Olympic Stadium in Sochi, Russia, will host the opening and closing ceremonies of the 2014 Winter Olympics. Soccer matches will be held there during the 2018 World Cup.*

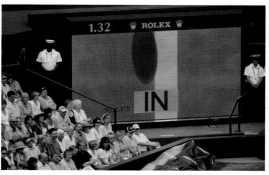

▲ *At major tennis events such as Wimbledon, large screens show computer-generated replays.*

Future stadiums will be wired for information technology (IT). Spectators will be able to watch the action on screens all over the stadium. They will also be able to download information and video clips to mobile telephones.

Glossary

amphitheater
A building, which is usually circular or oval, in which tiers of seats rise from a central open arena.

bedrock
Solid rock underneath the surface soil.

canyon
A long, narrow valley with steep sides.

compacted
Compressed or squashed together.

concourse
A wide hallway or corridor, or a large space where several pathways or corridors meet.

concrete
A building material made by mixing sand, gravel, cement, and water.

dredger
A ship used to dig sand, gravel, or silt from the bed of a river, lake, or sea.

earthquake
Shaking and vibration of the Earth's surface caused by movement along a fault.

foundation
The lowest part of a structure. The foundations of a building bear the structure's weight and are normally below ground level.

generator
A machine used to change motion into electricity.

grout
Thin mortar used to fill cracks and crevices.

hurricane
A tropical storm with winds that blow at more than 75 miles per hour (12 kilometers per hour).

hydroelectricity
Electricity that is produced using moving water to drive a turbine. The turbine powers a generator.

levee
An embankment or wall built to hold water back.

pile
A concrete or steel column that is driven down into the ground to form the foundation of a building or other structure.

powerhouse
The part of a dam where electricity is generated.

reinforced concrete
Concrete strengthened by steel bars.

reservoir
An artificial lake used for storing water.

stadium
A large structure where sports are played, with a playing surface surrounded by thousands of seats for spectators.

tier
One of two or more layers, one above the other. Tiered seating is rows of seats, one above another.

tower crane
A large crane, fixed to the ground on a concrete base, which is used to build tall structures.

tremor
A small earthquake.

turbine
A shaft or wheel with blades around the edge. When a liquid or gas flows through the blades, the turbine spins like a windmill in the breeze.

Top 10 biggest stadiums by capacity

Stadium	Location	Capacity
1. May Day Stadium	Pyongyang, North Korea	150,000
2. Salt Lake Stadium	Kolkata, India	120,000
3. Aztec Stadium	Mexico City, Mexico	115,000
4. Michigan Stadium	Michigan, USA	109,901
5. Beaver Stadium	Pennsylvania, USA	107,283
6. Neyland Stadium	Tennessee, USA	102,455
7. Ohio Stadium	Ohio, USA	102,329
8. Bryant–Denny Stadium	Alabama, USA	101,821
9. Darrell K Royal Stadium	Texas, USA	100,119
10. Melbourne Cricket Ground	Melbourne, Australia	100,018

Take it further

Design your own sports stadium. What would it look like? How would you make it look different than other stadiums?

Most scientists believe that air pollution caused by burning fossil fuels (coal, oil, and natural gas) is changing the world's climate. Clean electricity produced by methods such as hydroelectric plants does not add to this problem. Find out which countries make the most hydroelectricity.

Think about what the pyramids might have looked like if the ancient Egyptians had been able to use modern materials such as concrete, steel, plastic, and glass. Would they have been a different shape?

Useful websites

www.arizona-leisure.com/hoover-dam-building.html
Find out more about the building of the Hoover Dam.

www.london2012.com/webcams/
Watch the video clips to track the progess of the construction of stadiums for the London Olympics.

Website information is correct at time of going to press. However, the publishers cannot accept liability for any information or links found on third-party websites.

Index